The Ugly Duckling

Monica Hughes
Illustrated by Christina Bretschneider

Once upon a time Mother duck had some ducklings.

The ducklings grew and grew.
But one duckling grew too big.

Mother duck said, “Go away!
You are too big and too ugly.
You do not belong here.”

Poor Ugly Duckling!

He was so sad.

He went to see Hen.

Hen said, “Go away!
You are too big and too ugly.
You do not belong here.”

Poor Ugly Duckling!

He was so, so sad.

He went to see Cat.

Cat said, “Go away!
You are too big and too ugly.
You do not belong here.”

Poor Ugly Duckling!

He was so very sad.

He did not belong anywhere.

But then Ugly Duckling saw Swan.
He said, "I do not belong anywhere.
I am too big and too ugly."

Swan said, “You are **not** too big.
You are **not** ugly.”

"You are a swan!
And you belong here with us!"